Native Americans and the New American Government

Treaties and Promises

Kurt Ray

ROSEN CLASSROOM
PRIMARYSOURCE™

Rosen Classroom Books & Materials™
New York

Published in 2004 by The Rosen Publishing Group, Inc.
29 East 21st Street, New York, NY 10010

Library of Congress Cataloging-in-Publication Data

Ray, Kurt.
Native Americans and the new American government: treaties
and promises / by Kurt Ray. — 1st ed.
    p. cm. — (Life in the new American nation)
Summary: Discusses the treaties and battles between Native Americans and settlers of European descent during the early years of the United States, as well as the government's effort to end the violence by creating reservations. Includes bibliographical references and index.
ISBN 0-8239-4035-7 (lib. bdg.)
ISBN 0-8239-4253-8 (pbk. bdg.)
6-pack ISBN 0-8239-4266-X
1. Indians of North America—Government relations—Juvenile literature.
2. Indians of North America—Wars—Juvenile literature. [1. Indians of North America—Government relations. 2. Indians of North America—Wars. 3. Indians, Treatment of.] I. Title. II. Series.
E93.R29 2004
323.1'197073'09—dc21

2002152852

Manufactured in the United States of America

Cover (left): This is a painting of Andrew Jackson.
Cover (right): A photo of North American Indians

Photo Credits: Cover photo (left), pp. 5, 7, 10, 11, 16, 19, 21, 26 © Hulton/Archive/Getty Images; Cover photo (right), pp. 1, 20, 25 © Library of Congress; p. 15 © National Archives and Records Administration.

Designer and Photo Researcher: Nelson Sá; Editor: Eliza Berkowitz

Contents

Introduction

Some experts believe there were as many as fifteen million people living in North America before the year 1500. Native Americans were skilled artists, warriors, hunters, and farmers. Most tribes lived in one region. They moved within that area when the seasons changed. Sometimes they moved in order to follow the animals they hunted as a food supply.

Native American life was built around the community of the tribe. Property and possessions were shared by anyone who needed to use them. Decisions were made by everyone in the group, including women and young people. Native Americans did not have a formal religion, but they believed in the Great Spirit who provided for their needs. They believed that the land they lived on belonged to everyone. Though each tribe knew that there were other tribes of people in North America, they did not know about people from other parts of the world.

This is a photograph of a replica of the *Pinta*, one of Christopher Columbus's ships that set sail from Spain in search of a new route to Asia. Instead of finding a new route to Asia, Columbus landed on an island in what is now known as the Americas. Columbus is often credited with the discovery of the Americas, although native people had been living on the land for centuries.

Until the late fifteenth century, Europeans knew much about their own continent and a little about Africa and Asia. They had no idea that the continent of North America existed. That changed in 1492 when the European explorer Christopher Columbus set foot on an island in the Bahamas. Columbus was searching for an ocean route to Asia. He believed his ships had reached the country of India. He named the islands he found the Indies.

Chapter 1 A Clash of Cultures

Columbus's arrival in the Indies also marked the arrival of European culture and values. European culture included ideas of individual ownership and private property. Land and possessions were things to be bought and sold. Individual Europeans owned houses, money, and clothing. Wealthy Europeans even owned other human beings who worked for them as slaves. Europeans thought that people who lived more primitively than they did were "savages." In European minds, killing and enslaving savage people were necessary parts of expanding the European empire.

This is an engraving by F. Bartolozzi based on a drawing that was done by B. West in the 1500s. In this scene, a Native American leader is shown with Christopher Columbus. The arrival of European settlers changed the way the Native Americans were used to living. Their land was taken away, and they were forced to defend themselves against the settlers. This went on for many years.

Columbus called the native people "Indians," incorrectly believing that he had discovered islands near the country of India. In fact, Columbus was somewhere in the Bahamas. His name for the natives stuck, however, and for the next several centuries the native people of both North and South America were known as Indians.

Columbus claimed the land he found in the name of Spain, even though he knew that people already lived on the island. He forced some of those natives to return with him to Europe. Once there, they were converted to the Christian religion and put to work as slaves. Columbus saw nothing wrong with these actions. Like most Europeans at the time, he believed it was his right to treat "savage" races in this way.

Columbus's visit to the Indies began an era of European invasion of Native American lands. For Native Americans, each wave of European settlers brought disease and death. Native Americans offered peace and friendship to European visitors. In return, their land was stolen. Their villages were burned and their people were killed. In a very short period of time, most Native American culture was completely destroyed.

Early American Encounters

Chapter 2

Native Americans were shocked to see European settlers arriving in large ships during the 1500s. They were confused by European clothing and interested in the metal weapons the men carried. Native Americans frequently approached the settlers peacefully. Europeans, however, were scared of the dark-skinned people and often lashed out at them.

In 1585, an Englishman named Richard Greenville arrived in North America, near what is now the state of Virginia. Greenville had friendly relations with Native Americans from a nearby village. Soon after his arrival, though, Greenville learned that a silver cup had been stolen from the English by one of the Native Americans. Greenville and his men killed all the Native Americans and burned their village.

A few years later, English settlers founded Jamestown, Virginia. During a terrible winter in 1610, the English were unable to feed themselves. They began to starve. Some of the settlers left Jamestown. They

This is a painting of the village of Jamestown, Virginia. Jamestown was founded in 1607 and became the first British settlement in North America. It was a place where settlers and Native Americans lived very close to one another. Relations between settlers and Native Americans were not always bad. In fact, friendly relations were often formed.

moved into a Native American village where they were fed and cared for. When winter was over, the leaders of Jamestown went to the Native American leader, Powhatan. They asked him to return the settlers who were living with his people. Powhatan refused. The English responded by burning his village. They also

This is a painting of settlers and Native Americans in Jamestown. Jamestown is the site of one of many battles between the Native Americans and the European settlers. It started as a friendly meeting between the settlers and the natives. It ended in bloodshed after a Native American leader refused to return settlers to one of the leaders of Jamestown.

murdered one of Powhatan's wives and drowned her children.

Even without using violence, Europeans brought death to Native American tribes. Settlers from England, France, Spain, and the Netherlands brought common European illnesses with them, including smallpox and typhoid fever. Native Americans had never been exposed to such illnesses. Their bodies were unable to adapt quickly enough to protect them from getting sick. As a result, many of them died. In 1567, an outbreak of typhoid fever killed more than two million Native Americans. As many as ten million Native Americans died of disease during the first hundred years of European settlement in North America.

By 1600, it was clear to Native American tribes that the white settlers were not going to leave. Europeans did not move with the changing of the seasons. Instead, they built small towns and forts and stayed in one place. Native Americans realized that European settlements were causing long-term problems for their own people. They began to search for solutions.

The Trouble with Treaties   Chapter 3

Treaties are agreements between different groups or individuals. During the European settlement of North America, treaties were used to acquire land from Native American tribes. Usually, a treaty reflected an exchange of money for a piece of land. Sometimes a treaty was an agreement for one group to protect the other.

During the early 1600s, the Pilgrims left England and sailed to North America. They established a settlement in what is now Massachusetts. The settlement, Plymouth, was in the middle of a territory where the Wampanoag tribe lived. In 1621, the governor of Plymouth made a treaty with the Wampanoag chief, Massasoit. In the treaty, the

Pilgrims and Native Americans agreed to protect each other from outside forces. The Wampanoags also agreed to give up a portion of the land they lived on to the Pilgrims.

The two groups remained friendly for many years. Wampanoags taught the Pilgrims how to farm the land. They showed the Pilgrims how to hunt for seafood on the Massachusetts coast. The Pilgrims taught the Wampanoags how to fire European guns. Massasoit continued to make more treaties with the English. In each treaty, the Wampanoags gave up more and more pieces of land. Thousands of English settlers arrived to live there.

After Massasoit's death, his son, Metacom, became chief of the Wampanoags. Metacom was worried that Wampanoags had given up too much land during his father's life. The English began making unfair laws, like forcing the Wampanoags to give up all their weapons. Metacom refused. In 1675, he led the Wampanoags in a battle against the English settlers. He hoped to drive the English away for good.

At first the Wampanoags were successful in their attacks on English villages. Soon, however, English

Duplicate.

In the Name of the most Holy & undivided Trinity.

This is the Treaty of Paris, which was created in 1783. It divided up land in the New World that belonged to the French. Although Native Americans had lived on the land for years, this treaty did not leave them anything.

15

soldiers were brought in from other colonies to protect the settlers. Eventually Metacom and more than three thousand of his followers were killed. The English cut off Metacom's head and stuck it on a post at Plymouth, where it stayed as a warning to other Native Americans.

As European settlements continued to grow in North America, so did the fighting between England, Spain, and France. Each of these countries had control of large territories in North America, but they all wanted even more. Native Americans found themselves caught in the middle of these growing tensions. At every turn, Native

This is a picture of the Ottowa Indian chief, Pontiac, from around 1760. Pontiac is remembered for organizing a resistance to the settlers, which is called Pontiac's War. Pontiac was an ally of the French during the French and Indian War. He himself signed a peace treaty in July 1766, shortly before he was stabbed and killed by a fellow Native American.

Americans were forced to fight for land or sign treaties with Europeans that agreed to give away their land for small amounts of money or weapons.

The French and Indian War began in 1754 when French settlers built a fort on land the English claimed they owned. Native Americans fought on both sides of the war. Fighting with the English were the Six Nations of the Iroquois: Mohawks, Oneidas, Onondagas, Cayugas, Senecas, and Tuscaroras. These six tribes all spoke the language known as Iroquois. Fighting with the French were many tribes as well: Miamis, Menominees, Ottowas, Shawnees, and Hurons. The war dragged on for ten years and finally ended in 1763.

In a document called the Treaty of Paris, France agreed to give all of its land east of the Mississippi River to England. It gave all its land west of the Mississippi to Spain. Though Native Americans fought on both sides of the war, no consideration was given to their land rights. North America was divided between the three European countries as though the native tribes had never lived there.

Chapter 4

The Northwest Ordinance and the Indian Removal Act

In 1776, the American Revolutionary War began. Native Americans were again divided. The Iroquois nation split, with most tribes fighting for the British and other tribes fighting for the American colonists. When the war ended, the American colonists had won. For a brief time, it seemed that some of the Native American interests would be protected.

President George Washington was careful to remember Native American rights as plans were made for America's expansion. His government created the Northwest Ordinance, which stated that "the utmost good faith shall always be observed toward the Indians; their land and their property shall never be taken from them without

George Washington is pictured here with British General Charles Cornwallis, his enemy during the Revolutionary War. Cornwallis eventually surrendered and the Americans won independence. After America won, Washington tried to protect Native American land by creating the Northwest Ordinance, though it was hard to enforce and was not always observed.

their consent." Unfortunately, Washington's new government had no way of enforcing the ordinance. American settlers were greedy for land, and they continued to take it by force.

Another president, Andrew Jackson, was famous for killing Native Americans during the War of 1812. During that war, Jackson fought and won battles against the Creek tribe in Tennessee. After Jackson's men killed more than eight hundred Creek warriors, he crafted the Treaty of Fort Jackson. The treaty forced the Creeks and other tribes to give up most of their land in neighboring

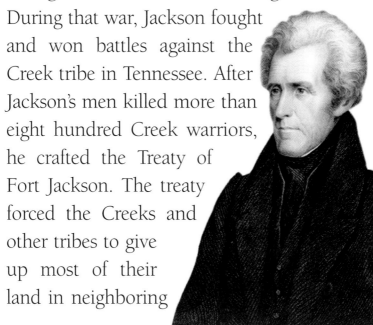

This is an illustration of Andrew Jackson, drawn from life and engraved by James Barton Longacre. Andrew Jackson is remembered for his cruel treatment of Native Americans during his presidency. He forced them to give up their land and he took many lives.

Alabama. Southern farmers quickly claimed the land. Many Native Americans were then forced to work as slaves on land where they had once lived freely.

During Jackson's presidency, Congress passed harsh laws that stripped Native Americans of their few remaining land rights. The most harmful of these laws was the Indian Removal Act of 1830. The Indian Removal Act forced all tribes to give up their land east of the Mississippi River. In exchange, they were to move to land that is now the state of Oklahoma. The area became known as

This is a picture of Major Ridge, a Native American from north Georgia. He is remembered for siding with the settlers and becoming hated by the people in his tribe. He rose to the rank of major during the Creek War. He was eventually killed for signing a treaty in 1835.

Native Americans were in a terrible position when it came to making treaties. Treaties were always written in French, English, or Spanish. Few Native Americans could read these languages. This meant that settlers could tell Native Americans one thing, while writing something different in a treaty.

There were even occasions when Americans served alcohol so that a Native American chief would be too drunk to understand the treaty he was signing. Americans would claim the treaty was valid because a Native American leader had signed it. Members of the tribe would be angered by a decision that had been made without their approval.

Indian Territory. Some American lawmakers opposed the act, but President Jackson quickly signed it into law.

Over the next twenty years, more than one hundred thousand Native Americans were forced to move to Indian Territory. Some walked or rode on horseback. Others were marched at gunpoint, forced by American soldiers to walk in chains. The Cherokee tribe was forced to march from Georgia to Oklahoma in 1838. More than four thousand Cherokees died along the journey. The path they followed became known as the Trail of Tears.

Reduced to Reservations

Development of the American West continued a violent pattern of American settlers seizing Native American lands. Entire tribes were wiped out by starvation as more and more settlers hunted buffalo that Native Americans depended on for food. Many Native Americans died in battles with U.S. soldiers who were brought in to protect settlers. Even tribes who tried to make peace with the United States were killed in terrible attacks.

During the late 1800s, the U.S. government tried to end the violence by setting aside small portions of land that would be reserved for Native American use. These "reservations" were often sections of land that were of no use to American settlers. By letting a tribe live on a reservation, the federal government agreed to take care of many of the tribe's needs. In exchange, the tribe agreed to live within the borders of the reservation. They gave up their rights to any other land.

The government provided for basic needs on each reservation. Schools, barns, and medical facilities were built. Financial assistance was provided. Churches were often built with the purpose of converting Native Americans to Christianity. Unfortunately, the creation of reservations was a poor solution to the problems faced by Native Americans. No consideration was given to their beliefs or traditions.

In 1887, Congress passed the General Allotment Act, or Dawes Act, which intended to split reservation land equally among Native Americans living there. Congress hoped that giving each Native American a small portion of land would encourage him to become a successful independent farmer. The act was a terrible failure. Native Americans still believed that land was to be used collectively. Though the act split the reservations up for private ownership, many

This is a 1909 photograph of a Cherokee Indian reservation in North Carolina. Reservations started when Congress passed the Allotment Act, giving Native Americans their own pieces of land. Unfortunately, this resulted in reservation land getting smaller, as Native Americans sold off their land to settlers. It wasn't until the 1930s that reservations were improved.

Native Americans sold off their individual pieces to American settlers. As a result, the small amount of land provided to reservations got even smaller.

Reservation life was full of problems. Many people were not well educated. Tribes also faced high rates of illness and alcoholism, a disease in which a person is addicted to drinking alcohol. The government agency in charge of reservations, the Bureau of Indian Affairs (BIA), was accused of mishandling money and supplies. It was not until the 1930s that a BIA official, John Collier, tried to change things.

Collier had great respect for Native American traditions. He helped set up a fund to buy back reservation land that had been sold off as a result of the Allotment

This is a photograph of John Collier taken in the 1940s. Collier, here with two Native Americans, is well known for helping Native Americans regain some of the land they had lost to settlers. By helping Native Americans improve reservations, he helped protect Native American culture. Many consider him to be a friend to the Native Americans.

Act. He allowed tribes to create their own rules for people living on reservations. He asked Congress to create a special division of the court system to help Native Americans solve their disagreements with the U.S. government. Not all of his plans were successful. Still, Collier's efforts helped Native Americans realize that they were not powerless.

Since the 1930s, Native Americans have made some progress in protecting their land and culture.

Members of many tribes fought as American soldiers in World War II. Many have left reservations to live their lives in cities and other regions. Many tribes have been successful in suing the U.S. government for stealing their land from them. With the money from these lawsuits, some tribes have created businesses that support the entire tribe.

More than 250 Native American reservations exist in the United States today. The people who live there still face challenges from outsiders who would like to take their land. They still face high rates of poverty and discrimination.

Hopefully, there will come a time when Native Americans receive the support and respect that have been denied them for many years. Until that time, the surviving tribes are fighting to preserve their culture and traditions.

Glossary

collectively (cuh-LEK-tiv-lee) Operating as a group.

colonist (KAH-luh-nist) Someone living in a new place who still has connections to his or her old country.

continent (KON-tin-ent) One of the seven large landmasses on Earth.

convert (kun-VERT) To change someone's belief to a different belief.

culture (KUL-chur) The beliefs and traditions of a certain group of people.

discrimination (dih-skrih-mih-NAY-shun) The act of treating a person poorly because of his or her differences.

era (AIR-uh) A period of time.

expansion (ek-SPAN-shun) The process of adding to something to make it larger.

expert (EK-spert) A person who is very knowledgeable about a subject.

fort (FORT) A place that can be defended against an enemy.

invasion (in-VAY-shun) The act of entering and attacking a place.

ordinance (ORD-nents) A law.

outbreak (OWT-brayk) The sudden occurrence or eruption of a disease.

possessions (POH-zeh-shunz) Things that are owned or occupied.

poverty (PAH-ver-tee) The state of being poor; having no money.

primitive (PRIH-muh-tiv) Something in its early stages; people who are not industrialized.

savage (SA-vij) Wild and ferocious.

settler (SET-ler) A person who makes his or her home in a new country or territory.

starvation (star-VAY-shun) The state of having no food to eat.

tribe (TRYB) A group of people sharing a common background and traditions.

violence (VY-ih-lents) Rough or harmful action.

Web Sites

Due to the changing nature of Internet links, the Rosen Publishing Group, Inc., has developed an online list of Web sites related to the subject of this book. This site is updated regularly. Please use this link to access the list:

http://www.rosenlinks.com/lnan/nanag

Primary Source Image List

Page 1: Photograph of Native Americans in North America, taken in 1908 by Edward S. Curtis.
Page 5: Photograph of a *Pinta* replica, taken in 1988. Housed in Ships of Discovery at the Corpus Christi Museum of Science and History.
Page 7: Engraving by F. Bartolozzi after a drawing by B. West. Created in 1796.
Page 10: Painting by Sidney King. Housed in the Colonial National Historical Park Collections.
Page 15: The document "The Treaty of Paris" was created in 1783. It is housed in the National Archives and Records Administration building.
Page 19: Painting by Constantino Brumidi. Housed in the Hall of Representatives, Washington, D.C.
Page 20: An engraving of Andrew Jackson by James Barton Longacre made in 1840. Housed in the Stapleton Collection.
Page 21: Artist unknown but believed to have been Charles Bird King. Created in 1834. Housed in the Smithsonian.
Page 25: Photograph by H. W. Pelton, taken in 1909.
Page 26: Photograph of John Collier taken in 1935. Housed in the National Archives and Records Administration building.

Index

About the Author

Kurt Ray is a freelance author who has written many books for young adults. He lives in Bozeman, Montana, where he enjoys his passions for fly-fishing and the music of Artaud Filberto.